ALEXANDER THE GREAT

BOOK FOR CURIOUS KIDS

The Story of a Young King Who Changed the Course of History

MARK LYLANI

TABLE OF CONTENTS

INTRODUCTION

Alexander the Great was only 20 years old when he set out to conquer the world. From Greece to Egypt, Persia to India, his name became known across the lands, and his army achieved victories that would go down in history. But Alexander wasn't just a conqueror—he was a visionary who changed the course of the world and left a legacy that still influences us today.

In this book, we will explore the incredible journey of Alexander, from his early life in Macedonia to his epic campaigns that stretched across continents. Along the way, you'll discover what made him such a remarkable leader, how he inspired loyalty in his men, and how he overcame obstacles that seemed impossible to conquer.

Through his adventures, Alexander's life offers important lessons about ambition, leadership, perseverance, and thinking big. His story shows that with a clear goal and determination, challenges can be conquered, and great things can be achieved. As we follow Alexander's path, get ready to be inspired by his courage, his boldness, and his relentless drive to make the world a better place.

Let's begin the journey of one of history's greatest figures and see how his life can inspire your own adventures and dreams!

The Early Years

Imagine a palace filled with golden decorations, bustling servants, and the smell of rich feasts wafting through the air. This is where Alexander's incredible story begins. On a warm summer night in 356 BCE, in the city of Pella, Macedonia, a baby was born who would change the world. That baby was Alexander, the son of King Philip II and Queen Olympias. From the moment he took his first breath, his parents believed he was destined for greatness.

A Prince with Royal Blood

Alexander wasn't just any baby. He came from a line of kings, warriors, and legends. His father, King Philip II, was a brilliant leader who had transformed Macedonia into a powerful kingdom. Philip was known for his strategic mind and determination. Under his rule, the once-small kingdom became a force to be reckoned with in the ancient world.

Queen Olympias, Alexander's mother, was just as extraordinary. She was passionate, clever, and deeply spiritual. She often told Alexander stories about heroes, particularly the great warrior Achilles, who she said was one of their ancestors. Alexander grew up believing that he had a unique spark within him, and that spark fueled his dreams of doing amazing things.

Life in the Palace

Life in the royal palace was exciting and full of learning for young Alexander. As a prince, he had the best teachers, the finest clothes, and more opportunities than most children could dream of. But being royalty wasn't all about fun and luxury. From an early age,

Alexander was taught that his future would be filled with challenges, battles, and important decisions. He had to be ready.

King Philip believed that a strong mind was just as important as a strong body. He made sure Alexander was educated by the best scholars of the time. But before the famous philosopher Aristotle became his tutor, Alexander's learning began at home. He studied music, poetry, and history, as well as the skills needed to lead armies. By the time he was a young boy, Alexander was already learning how to inspire people and make tough choices.

A Horse Like No Other

One of the most famous stories from Alexander's childhood is about a horse named Bucephalus. This wasn't just any horse. Bucephalus was a massive, powerful animal with a wild and untamed spirit. No one could control him, not even the most skilled horse trainers in the kingdom. When Alexander was about 12 years old, he saw Bucephalus for the first time. The horse reared up and snorted angrily, scaring everyone around him.

King Philip shook his head. "This horse is useless," he said. "He's too wild." But Alexander had other ideas.

"Let me try," he said confidently. The king laughed but agreed to let his son give it a shot.

As Alexander approached Bucephalus, he noticed something that the others had missed. The horse wasn't angry; he was afraid of his own shadow. Slowly and calmly, Alexander turned Bucephalus to face the sun so that the shadow was behind him. Then, speaking softly, he climbed onto the horse's back. To everyone's amazement, Bucephalus didn't buck or rear. Instead, he stood still as if he trusted Alexander completely.

With a gentle nudge, Alexander urged the horse forward, and together they galloped across the field. The crowd erupted in cheers, and King Philip's eyes shone with pride.

"My son," he said, "you must find a kingdom big enough for your ambitions. Macedonia will not be enough."

From that day on, Bucephalus became Alexander's faithful companion. The bond between boy and horse was unbreakable, and they would go on to share countless adventures.

Lessons from a King and a Queen

Alexander's parents taught him more than just lessons about ruling and bravery. King Philip showed him the importance of strategy, whether it was on the battlefield or in the royal court. He often took Alexander to watch military drills and explained the tactics behind his victories. Young Alexander soaked up this knowledge like a sponge, eager to apply it himself one day.

Queen Olympias, on the other hand, taught him to dream big and to believe in his own greatness. She surrounded him with stories of heroes who overcame impossible odds. Her favorite tales were about Achilles, the Greek hero of the Trojan War. She told Alexander that Achilles wasn't just a character in a story—he was family. These stories made Alexander feel that he was part of something bigger, something legendary.

A Future Full of Possibilities

By the time Alexander was a teenager, he was already showing signs of the leader he would become. He was curious, brave, and determined to leave his mark on the world. Every lesson, every story, and every experience shaped him into someone who believed that anything was possible.

The early years of Alexander's life weren't just about learning facts or practicing skills. They were about building the foundation for a dream that would change history. With a father who taught him strength and strategy, a mother who filled his mind with heroic tales, and a loyal horse by his side, Alexander's journey was just beginning.

Questions

- Where was Alexander the Great born, and who were his parents?

- What lesson did Alexander learn from taming Bucephalus?

- What kinds of stories did Queen Olympias share with Alexander, and why were they important to him?

- What did King Philip II teach Alexander about leadership and strategy?

- What did King Philip say after Alexander tamed Bucephalus?

The Education of a Prince

Alexander was no ordinary student. While most kids his age were learning basic skills or playing games, Alexander had the best teacher in the ancient world: Aristotle. Imagine having a classroom under the open sky, surrounded by trees, with a philosopher who could explain the stars and the workings of the human mind. This is how Alexander spent some of his most important years, learning lessons that would shape his future as a leader and conqueror.

A Teacher Like No Other

When Alexander turned 13, his father, King Philip II, decided it was time for the young prince to have a tutor who could teach him more than just the basics. King Philip wanted someone exceptional, someone who could prepare Alexander to rule not just Macedonia but perhaps the entire known world. That someone was Aristotle, one of the greatest thinkers of all time.

Aristotle wasn't just a regular teacher with a stack of scrolls. He was a man of deep wisdom who believed in asking big questions about life, the universe, and everything in between. When Aristotle arrived at the palace, he and Alexander hit it off instantly. The teacher saw the prince's curiosity and determination, and Alexander admired Aristotle's vast knowledge. Together, they created an incredible bond built on learning and discovery.

Lessons Under the Sky

Aristotle didn't teach Alexander in a stuffy classroom with stone walls. Instead, lessons often took place outdoors. In the gardens or under the shade of ancient trees, Aristotle taught Alexander about subjects most people hadn't even heard of. They talked about philosophy, which was all about asking why things were the way they were. They discussed science, learning about plants, animals, and even the stars that glittered in the night sky.

One day, Aristotle handed Alexander a frog and asked, "What do you think makes it move and live?" Alexander studied the frog carefully, asking questions and offering his thoughts. It wasn't about finding the right answer—it was about learning how to think deeply and critically.

Alexander also learned about literature, especially the epic poems of Homer. These stories about great heroes and their adventures filled Alexander with ideas about bravery and leadership. Aristotle encouraged him to see the lessons hidden within the tales, like the importance of courage, loyalty, and perseverance.

But it wasn't all books and scrolls. Alexander's education included lessons on warfare and strategy. His teacher explained the importance of outsmarting enemies and thinking creatively in battles. These lessons planted the seeds for Alexander's genius as a military commander later in life.

Big Questions and Bigger Dreams

Aristotle encouraged Alexander to think big. They often discussed ideas about the world beyond Macedonia. What lay beyond the mountains, rivers, and seas? Could a single leader unite many lands under one rule? These were the kinds of ideas that sparked Alexander's imagination. He began to dream not just of being a king but of being a ruler who could bring different cultures together.

One of Aristotle's most important lessons was about balance. He taught Alexander that a great leader needed to be strong yet kind, wise yet humble. This balance would help Alexander gain the trust of his people and inspire loyalty among his soldiers.

Books, Scrolls, and Curiosity

Aristotle introduced Alexander to books and scrolls filled with knowledge from all over the ancient world. They read about history, geography, and medicine. Alexander's favorite scrolls were about places far away—lands with towering pyramids, deserts of golden sand, and cities bustling with trade and ideas. These stories filled him with a sense of adventure and a hunger to explore.

"Knowledge," Aristotle told him one day, "is the greatest treasure a leader can have. With it, you can make decisions that change the world." Alexander took this advice to heart. He wasn't just learning facts; he was preparing for a future where those facts could guide his actions.

The Birth of a Visionary

By the time Alexander finished studying with Aristotle at age 16, he was more than just a prince—he was a young man with a vision. He didn't see borders and barriers; he saw opportunities to connect people and ideas. Every lesson Aristotle taught him, whether about the stars or the strategies of war, helped shape this vision.

Aristotle's influence stayed with Alexander throughout his life. The lessons in critical thinking, leadership, and curiosity became tools Alexander used in his incredible journey to change history. He carried these tools with him as he stepped into the world, ready to turn his dreams into reality.

A Foundation for Greatness

Alexander's education wasn't just about facts or skills; it was about building the foundation for greatness. With Aristotle as his guide, he learned to see the world in new ways. He wasn't just learning how to rule a kingdom—he was preparing to lead a world.

The bond between teacher and student left a lasting mark. Long after their lessons ended, Alexander would look back on these years as some of the most important in his life. Every question Aristotle asked, every story they read, and every strategy they discussed prepared Alexander to become one of the most remarkable leaders in history.

For Alexander, learning wasn't just a duty—it was an adventure. And with each passing day, he grew more eager to take what he had learned and turn it into action. The education of a prince wasn't easy, but for

Alexander, it was the key to unlocking his extraordinary potential.

Questions

- Who was Alexander's famous tutor, and why was he chosen?
- Where did Alexander often have his lessons, and why was this unusual?
- What kinds of subjects did Alexander study with Aristotle?
- What lesson about leadership did Aristotle emphasize to Alexander?
- How did Alexander's education shape his vision for the future?

First Taste of Power

Alexander was no ordinary teenager. By the time he was 16, while most kids might be worrying about school or chores, he was already stepping into the world of battles and leadership. With King Philip II, his father, leading one of the most powerful armies in Greece, it was only a matter of time before Alexander had his chance to shine. And when that moment came, he didn't just meet expectations—he smashed them.

Taking Command

In 340 BCE, Philip was preparing for yet another military campaign. But this time, he needed someone he could trust to take charge of Macedonia in his absence. To everyone's surprise, he handed the reins to Alexander. Imagine the responsibility—leading an entire kingdom while still a teenager! Alexander took this challenge head-on.

It wasn't long before trouble came knocking. A nearby tribe decided this was the perfect time to rebel, thinking they could take advantage of Philip's absence. But Alexander wasn't about to let that happen. He quickly assembled an army and marched out to face the threat. Using the skills he'd learned from years of watching his father, Alexander crushed the rebellion and secured the kingdom. It was his first taste of command, and he proved he was more than ready for the job.

The Battle of Chaeronea

Alexander's biggest test came two years later, in 338 BCE, during the Battle of Chaeronea. This wasn't just any skirmish—it was a massive clash between the Macedonian army and a coalition of Greek city-states, including Athens and Thebes. Philip led the army, but Alexander played a crucial role.

At just 18 years old, Alexander was given command of the left wing of the Macedonian army. This was a big deal because the left wing was one of the most important positions in battle. It was where the fiercest fighting often took place. Alexander, however, didn't flinch. He studied the battlefield carefully, noticing how the enemy lines moved and looking for weaknesses.

As the battle raged on, Alexander saw his opportunity. With a burst of energy, he led a cavalry charge straight into the enemy ranks. His strategy was brilliant—he didn't just charge blindly; he targeted a weak spot in the enemy's formation. The charge was so powerful and well-timed that it turned the tide of the entire battle. The coalition forces were thrown into chaos, and the Macedonians emerged victorious.

Alexander's actions at Chaeronea weren't just impressive; they were legendary. Even seasoned generals were amazed at his courage and tactical mind. For Philip, it was clear that his son wasn't just a promising prince—he was a born leader.

Father and Son

While Alexander and Philip were both strong and brilliant, their relationship wasn't always smooth. Philip was proud of his son's achievements, but he was also a king with his own ambitions. Sometimes, their strong personalities clashed. Alexander, with his youthful energy and bold ideas, didn't always see eye to eye with his father.

One story highlights their complex relationship. After the victory at Chaeronea, Philip held a huge celebration. As part of the festivities, he toasted Alexander's role in the battle. But later, when the celebrations got a bit too rowdy, Philip stumbled while trying to confront someone. Alexander, quick-witted as always, joked, "Look at the man who plans to conquer the world but can't even stand up straight!" It was a sharp comment, and it showed that Alexander wasn't afraid to speak his mind, even with his father.

Despite their differences, Philip and Alexander had a deep respect for each other. Philip saw the future of Macedonia in his son, and Alexander admired his father's ability to lead and strategize. Their relationship was a mix of admiration, rivalry, and the occasional disagreement—much like many families today.

Leadership in Action

What made Alexander's early leadership so remarkable was not just his bravery but also his ability to inspire others. Soldiers twice his age followed him without hesitation because they believed in his vision. He didn't lead from the back; he was always at the front, charging into danger alongside his men.

Alexander also had a way of connecting with people. He took the time to understand their struggles and made them feel like they were part of something bigger. Whether it was calming a frightened soldier or rallying his troops before a battle, Alexander had a gift for bringing out the best in those around him.

These early experiences shaped Alexander into the leader he would become. Every decision, every charge, and every victory taught him something new about himself and the world. By the time he turned 20, he wasn't just Philip's son or a promising young prince. He was a proven commander, ready to take on whatever challenges lay ahead.

The Road Ahead

The Battle of Chaeronea wasn't the end of Alexander's journey—it was just the beginning. The confidence he gained from these early victories gave him the courage to dream even bigger. He didn't just want to lead Macedonia; he wanted to leave a mark on history.

With each challenge, Alexander grew stronger, smarter, and more determined. The boy who had taken his first command at 16 was now a young man who had stood shoulder to shoulder with some of the greatest warriors of his time. And this was only the start of his incredible story.

Questions

- Who did King Philip leave in charge of Macedonia when he went on campaign?

- How did Alexander handle the rebellion while Philip was away?
- What role did Alexander play in the Battle of Chaeronea?
- Why did Alexander and Philip sometimes clash in their relationship?
- What qualities made Alexander a great leader at a young age?

The Rise of a King

In the year 336 BCE, an event happened that would change the course of history. King Philip II of Macedonia, a mighty ruler who had been building an empire, was assassinated. His death came as a huge shock to the world. But it also marked the beginning of a new era—one led by his son, Alexander.

At just 20 years old, Alexander was suddenly thrust into the role of king. Imagine that! A teenager becoming the ruler of a powerful kingdom with enemies all around. But Alexander was not afraid. He had been trained for this moment from a young age. His father, King Philip, had taught him how to lead, fight, and think like a king.

So, even though Alexander was young, he was ready to take on the world.

The First Challenge: Proving Himself

When Alexander became king, not everyone was excited about his rise to power. Some people doubted his abilities because he was so young. But Alexander wasn't going to sit around and wait for people to change their minds. Instead, he took action right away.

One of his first moves was to deal with some rebellious Greek city-states. The Greeks had always been proud of their independence, and with King Philip gone, some cities thought they could rebel and break away from Macedonia's control. The city of Thebes was one of the most powerful rebels.

But Alexander wasn't going to let that happen. He marched his army to Thebes and laid siege to the city. The battle was fierce, but Alexander's army was well-trained and prepared. In the end, Thebes fell, and Alexander made it clear to the rest of Greece that he was in charge. His victory sent a strong message: If you wanted to challenge Alexander, you would face the full force of his power.

Securing the Throne

Even though Alexander had proven himself by defeating Thebes, his rule was still not secure. There were still other rivals who didn't want to follow him, both inside and outside of Macedonia. Some of them were jealous of his rise to power, and others just didn't believe he could live up to his father's legacy.

One of his biggest challenges came from the Greek city-state of Athens. Athens had always been a leader among the Greek cities, and it wasn't too happy about Alexander's rise to power. But instead of rushing into battle with Athens, Alexander made a smart move: he used his diplomacy skills to calm things down. He convinced the city-states that his leadership was in their best interest and that he would bring stability to the region.

By the time Alexander finished dealing with the rebels and securing his throne, he had already shown that he was not just the son of a great king—he was a leader in his own right.

Uniting the Greek City-States

After securing his rule in Macedonia, Alexander faced his next challenge: uniting all of the Greek city-states under his control. While King Philip had been able to bring many of the Greek cities together, there were still some who resisted and wanted to stay independent. Alexander knew that if he wanted to build a lasting empire, he had to make sure that all of Greece was united.

But it wasn't easy. The Greek cities had a long history of rivalry and independence, and convincing them to work together was no simple task. However, Alexander was a master of both war and diplomacy. He used both force and persuasion to get the Greek city-states to agree to form a unified alliance under his leadership. This alliance would not only strengthen his rule but also prepare them for bigger challenges ahead—like the Persian Empire, one of the largest empires in the world at the time.

He called the Greek states together and presented them with an opportunity they couldn't refuse: by uniting with him, they could become stronger and face their enemies together. In the end, most of the cities agreed to join his alliance. Alexander had done it—he had unified Greece, and now, he was ready to take the next step on his journey to greatness.

A New Kind of King

Alexander's rise to the throne wasn't just about battles and wars. It was about his leadership. He wasn't just following in his father's footsteps—he was creating his own path. Alexander was not only a skilled warrior but also a smart strategist. He knew how to use both his strength and his mind to get what he wanted.

He made sure to treat his soldiers with respect, always leading from the front and sharing in their hardships. This earned him the loyalty of his army, which would follow him through thick and thin. But he also knew when to show kindness and diplomacy. Instead of ruling with fear, Alexander earned the respect of those around him. He showed that he was not just a king but a ruler who could inspire others to follow him.

At just 20 years old, Alexander had already proven that he was a force to be reckoned with. He had taken control of Macedonia, defeated powerful enemies, and unified the Greek city-states. His rise to power was not an easy one, but it was a journey that would eventually lead him to conquer the world.

And so, the story of Alexander the Great began—not as a young king with everything handed to him, but as a leader who fought for what he believed in and was willing to face any challenge that came his way.

But this was just the beginning. As Alexander looked to the horizon, he knew that the real adventure was still ahead of him. The Persian Empire loomed to the east, and Alexander was determined to take it on, one battle at a time. But for now, he had secured his place as the king of Macedonia and united Greece under his rule. And that was no small achievement.

This was the rise of a king—a young, ambitious ruler who was just beginning to carve out his legacy in the world. And little did anyone know, Alexander was about to become one of the greatest conquerors the world had ever seen. But that story is for another time.

Questions

- How did Alexander prove his strength as a leader after becoming king?
- What city did Alexander first attack to show his power after his father's assassination?
- What challenges did Alexander face when trying to unite the Greek city-states?
- How did Alexander earn the loyalty of his soldiers?

- Why did Alexander believe uniting Greece was important for his future plans?

The Campaign Against Persia Begins

After Alexander secured his rule in Macedonia and united the Greek city-states, he had one big dream in mind—conquering Persia. But why did he want to take on one of the largest empires in the world at the time?

Why Alexander Wanted to Conquer the Persian Empire

The Persian Empire was massive, stretching across a huge part of the world. It controlled lands from Egypt all the way to India, and its rulers were incredibly powerful. Alexander had heard stories of Persia's greatness from a young age. But he also knew that his father, King Philip II, had started planning to attack Persia before he was killed.

Alexander knew that defeating Persia would not only make him one of the most powerful kings in history but also fulfill his father's dream. Plus, Alexander was eager to prove himself. He wanted to show the world that he was just as capable of great victories as his father had been. But there was another reason—Alexander believed that by conquering Persia, he would be able to unite the Greek world and build an empire that could last for generations.

The Persian Empire had a history of conflict with the Greek city-states, and Alexander felt that by defeating Persia, he could right past wrongs and take back land that had been lost. He wasn't just fighting for land—he was fighting for a sense of justice and honor. His heart was set on bringing glory to Macedonia, but also to all of Greece.

The Big Decision: Crossing the Hellespont

After carefully planning his attack, Alexander gathered an army and prepared to march toward Persia. His first step was to cross the Hellespont, a narrow body of water that separates Europe from Asia. This was no small task. The Persian Empire lay on the other side of the Hellespont, and Alexander knew that this would be the start of a long and dangerous journey. But he was determined.

Now, you might be wondering: how did they cross the Hellespont? Well, at the time, there weren't any big bridges like we have today. Instead, Alexander's army had to use boats and ships to carry them across the water. But there was something else about the crossing that made it even more exciting.

As Alexander prepared to cross, he made a bold gesture. He had the Persian king's statue thrown into the sea, symbolizing that he was not afraid of Persia's power. It was like he was telling the Persian Empire, "I'm coming for you, and nothing can stop me!"

Once they crossed the Hellespont, Alexander and his army were officially on their way to face the mighty Persian Empire. The journey wasn't going to be easy, but Alexander was full of energy and courage, ready to lead his army into battle.

The First Major Victory: The Battle of Granicus

With the Hellespont behind them, Alexander's army marched into the Persian heartland. The first major battle came quickly—The Battle of Granicus, which would become an important turning point in his campaign. It took place near the Granicus River, and it was the first time Alexander would face the mighty Persian army on the battlefield.

The Persian forces were led by local satraps, or governors, who had gathered a large army to fight off the invaders. They thought they could stop Alexander in his tracks. After all, they had a powerful army and plenty of soldiers. But they didn't know who they were up against.

Alexander's army was well-trained and highly disciplined, and it was led by a king who knew how to fight. As the battle began, Alexander charged forward with his cavalry, riding straight into the Persian forces. It was a bold move, but it paid off. Alexander's cavalry was quick and strong, and they broke through the Persian lines.

The Persians were caught off guard by the speed and strength of Alexander's attack. They tried to regroup and fight back, but Alexander's soldiers were determined. The battle was fierce, but Alexander's forces won decisively. The Persian army was forced to retreat, and the victory was a huge boost to Alexander's morale.

The Battle of Granicus was Alexander's first major victory against the Persian Empire. It showed that he was not only capable of leading his army but also of defeating one of the most powerful empires in the world. But this was just the beginning of his campaign. Alexander knew that there would be more battles ahead and that his journey to conquer Persia was far from over.

The Importance of the Victory

The victory at Granicus was important for a few reasons. First, it showed that Alexander was ready to take on the mighty Persian Empire. It also helped boost the confidence of his soldiers, who now believed that they could conquer anything. But perhaps most importantly, it sent a strong message to the Persian Empire: Alexander was coming, and he wasn't going to stop until he had conquered everything in his path.

After the battle, Alexander continued to move forward, conquering cities and winning battles. His victory at Granicus was a key moment in his campaign, and it marked the start of what would become one of the greatest military achievements in history.

The Path Ahead

After the Battle of Granicus, Alexander didn't just sit back and relax. He knew that there was still a long road ahead of him. He had won his first victory, but the Persian Empire was vast, and it wasn't going to fall easily. But Alexander wasn't afraid of challenges. He had faced obstacles his whole life and had always come out on top.

With his army by his side, Alexander marched onward. He faced more battles, more obstacles, and more challenges. But every time he won, his fame spread, and his army grew stronger. He didn't just fight for glory—he fought to change the world. Along the way, he inspired others to follow him.

The campaign against Persia had only just begun, but Alexander was on a path that would lead him to become one of the greatest conquerors the world has ever known. He had already taken his first steps into Persia, and his journey was far from over. Each victory was a step closer to realizing his dream of building an empire that would last for centuries. But for now, he could take a moment to enjoy the sweet taste of victory at the Battle of Granicus—and look forward to the challenges ahead.

Questions

- Why did Alexander want to conquer the Persian Empire?

- How did Alexander's army cross the Hellespont?
- What bold action did Alexander take before crossing the Hellespont?
- What happened during the Battle of Granicus?
- How did Alexander's victory at Granicus affect his soldiers and the Persian Empire?

Conquering Asia Minor

After his stunning victory at the Battle of Granicus, Alexander's path to glory was clear. The mighty Persian Empire still stood in his way, but Alexander wasn't one to back down. He had a plan, and he was ready to put it into action. This time, he wasn't just relying on his sword and his cavalry; he would use his sharp mind and diplomacy to outsmart his enemies and gain new allies.

Alexander marched his army into Asia Minor, the land we now call Turkey. This was a crucial step in his journey because it was the first part of Persia's empire that he needed to conquer before he could push deeper into their territory. But Asia Minor wasn't just about fighting—it was also about making decisions that would affect the entire future of his campaign.

Strategy and Diplomacy

While Alexander's army was made up of soldiers who were excellent at fighting, Alexander knew that victory wasn't just about strength. He also understood the importance of making smart choices, building alliances, and using his skills in diplomacy to gain the support of local leaders. His strategy was a combination of brilliant fighting tactics and a way with people that won him friends as well as enemies.

As he moved through Asia Minor, Alexander didn't always have to fight. Instead of attacking every city he came across, he sometimes offered the cities the chance to join him willingly. When a city surrendered without a fight, he treated them with respect and fairness. He didn't want to destroy everything in his path; he wanted to unite the people of Asia Minor under his rule. By showing kindness to those who chose to support him, Alexander built a network of allies who would help him in his future battles.

However, not everyone was willing to accept Alexander's leadership. Some cities, especially those that had been under Persian control for a long time, resisted. When those cities didn't give in, Alexander used his military power to defeat them. His army moved quickly and decisively, showing the people of Asia Minor that it was better to join him than to stand against him.

The Gordian Knot: A Legendary Puzzle

One of the most famous moments of Alexander's campaign happened in Phrygia, a kingdom in Asia Minor. There was a legend there about an incredible puzzle: the Gordian Knot. This knot was tied by the legendary King Gordius, and it was so complicated that no one had been able to untie it. It was said that whoever could unravel the knot would become the ruler of all of Asia.

When Alexander arrived in the city, he was told about the Gordian Knot and the legend surrounding it. He decided to take a look for himself. The knot was huge, tangled, and seemed impossible to untie. Many people had tried and failed, but Alexander wasn't just anyone. He believed that if something was worth doing, it was worth doing in his own bold way.

Instead of carefully trying to untie the knot like everyone before him, Alexander did something unexpected. He took his sword and cut the knot in half. Some people were shocked by his boldness, but Alexander simply said, "It doesn't matter how you untie it, as long as it's done." His action proved that he wasn't afraid to make big decisions and take risks, even if they didn't follow the rules. And, as the legend promised, Alexander was destined to rule over all of Asia.

The Gordian Knot became a symbol of Alexander's power and his belief that obstacles could be overcome with bold actions. It wasn't just about solving problems the usual way—it was about thinking outside the box and being confident in your choices.

Inspiring Loyalty

As Alexander continued his conquest of Asia Minor, he not only faced the challenges of battle but also the challenge of keeping his men loyal and motivated. Leading an army across vast lands and through many battles wasn't easy, and Alexander knew that his soldiers needed more than just orders—they needed to feel connected to the cause.

One of the things that made Alexander such a great leader was his ability to inspire loyalty among his men. He didn't act like a distant king who only cared about his own power. Instead, he lived and fought alongside his soldiers. Alexander shared their hardships, ate the same food, and slept in the same conditions. When it was time for a tough battle, he was always in the front, charging ahead with his cavalry. His bravery made his soldiers believe in him and trust that he would lead them to victory.

But loyalty wasn't just about following orders. Alexander knew how to make his men feel valued. After every victory, he celebrated with his soldiers, sharing the glory of their achievements. He praised them for their courage and made sure that they knew they were an important part of his success. As a result, Alexander's army was one of the most motivated and loyal in history.

He also built a strong relationship with the local people. Many of the cities he conquered in Asia Minor were reluctant at first, but Alexander was known for his ability to make peace with those who surrendered. He didn't want to be seen as a tyrant; he wanted to be seen as a just and fair ruler. By treating the local people with respect and giving them the freedom to live as they wished (as long as they didn't resist his rule), Alexander was able to gain their trust and make his empire stronger.

In return, the local people often welcomed Alexander as a leader who could bring peace and prosperity. His ability to connect with both his soldiers and the local people helped him build a strong, united empire that was ready for the challenges ahead.

Moving Forward

By the time Alexander had conquered most of Asia Minor, his reputation was growing.

He had won battle after battle, and cities were falling under his control. His army was loyal, and the people he ruled over were beginning to support him. But Alexander wasn't done yet. He still had much to achieve.

His next goal was to push deeper into the heart of the Persian Empire. He had already defeated some of the Persian forces, but he knew that the biggest challenges were yet to come. As he continued his journey, his army faced more dangers, more enemies, and more obstacles. But Alexander was ready for whatever came next.

With his mind sharp, his soldiers loyal, and his strategy in place, Alexander was preparing to take on even bigger battles. The conquest of Asia Minor was just the beginning, and nothing could stand in the way of the young king who was destined to change the world.

As Alexander moved through Asia Minor, he showed that being a great leader wasn't just about winning battles—it was about thinking strategically, inspiring loyalty, and using wisdom and diplomacy to build a stronger empire. He wasn't just a conqueror; he was a leader who understood the importance of people and relationships. His bold move with the Gordian Knot and his ability to connect with his soldiers and the local people proved that he wasn't just a warrior—he was a king who knew how to unite and inspire those around him. And with each victory, Alexander's dreams of ruling the world grew closer.

Questions

- How did Alexander use diplomacy to gain support from cities in Asia Minor?
- What did the Gordian Knot legend say about the person who could untie it?

- What bold action did Alexander take to solve the Gordian Knot puzzle?

- How did Alexander inspire loyalty among his soldiers during his campaign?

- Why did many local people in Asia Minor welcome Alexander as their leader?

The Battle of Issus

After his sweeping victories in Asia Minor, Alexander and his army marched forward, facing the mighty Persian Empire head-on. His target? King Darius III, the ruler of Persia. Alexander was no stranger to challenges, and this time, the stakes were higher than ever. The clash at Issus would prove to be one of the most decisive battles of his journey.

A Narrow Battlefield

King Darius III commanded a massive army, one that dwarfed Alexander's forces in size. Darius was confident. He believed that Alexander would finally crumble under the weight of Persia's sheer numbers. But

Alexander had something even more powerful than numbers—he had strategy, courage, and a sharp mind that could see opportunities others couldn't.

The two armies met near the narrow plains of Issus. The location turned out to be a brilliant advantage for Alexander. Why? Because Darius' massive army had little room to move in the confined space. Instead of spreading out and overwhelming Alexander's smaller force, the Persians were forced into tight quarters where they couldn't use their full strength.

Alexander knew this was his chance to outmaneuver Darius. He arranged his army in a formation that played to their strengths. His phalanx—a tight group of heavily armed soldiers—formed the center, while his cavalry, led by Alexander himself, took positions on the sides. It was a setup that allowed Alexander to control the flow of the battle, even against overwhelming odds.

Outmaneuvering Darius

When the battle began, Darius sent his forces forward, expecting an easy victory. But Alexander had other plans. He led a bold cavalry charge straight at the Persian left flank, catching them off guard. His soldiers moved with precision, pushing the Persians back and creating chaos in their ranks.

Meanwhile, Alexander's phalanx advanced steadily, holding the center of the battlefield. The Persian soldiers, who were used to relying on their numbers, struggled to hold their ground. Alexander's army worked like a well-oiled machine, with every move calculated to weaken the Persian forces.

However, the most daring part of Alexander's strategy was his personal charge toward Darius himself. Spotting the Persian king in his grand chariot, Alexander led his cavalry straight into the heart of the

Persian army, aiming to strike fear into their leader. Darius, seeing Alexander's ferocity and the chaos spreading among his troops, panicked. Instead of standing his ground, Darius fled the battlefield, leaving his soldiers to face Alexander's unstoppable force.

A King's Family Captured

As Darius escaped, Alexander's soldiers stumbled upon an unexpected prize: Darius' family. The Persian king's wife, mother, and children had been left behind in the royal camp. It was a stunning turn of events. Capturing the family of a king was more than just a victory—it was a huge blow to Darius' pride and authority.

But what Alexander did next showed the kind of leader he was. Instead of treating Darius' family harshly, Alexander treated them with respect and dignity. He ensured they were cared for and protected, earning admiration from both his soldiers and the Persian people. By showing compassion to his enemy's family, Alexander sent a powerful message: he wasn't just a conqueror—he was a ruler who valued honor.

This act of kindness also helped Alexander politically. Many Persian cities began to see him not as a ruthless invader but as a leader they could trust. It was another example of how Alexander combined strategy and diplomacy to strengthen his position.

A Turning Point

The Battle of Issus wasn't just another victory for Alexander—it was a turning point in his campaign against Persia. Defeating Darius and capturing his family showed the world that Alexander was a force to be reckoned with. Word of the battle spread quickly, and people across Persia began to question Darius' ability to protect them.

For Alexander, this victory wasn't just about defeating an enemy—it was about building momentum. Each win brought him closer to his ultimate goal of conquering the entire Persian Empire. The Battle of Issus proved that Alexander wasn't just lucky or bold—he was a brilliant strategist who could outthink even the most powerful kings.

The Road Ahead

After the battle, Alexander didn't stop to celebrate for long. He knew that Darius was still out there, gathering more troops and preparing for another showdown. But Alexander wasn't worried. He had proven that his army could face anything, no matter the odds.

As they marched further into Persia, Alexander's soldiers carried with them the confidence of victory. They had seen their leader outsmart a king and send a massive army into retreat. They believed in

Alexander's vision and were ready to follow him wherever he led.

The Battle of Issus had changed everything. It wasn't just a victory on the battlefield—it was a moment that showed the world who Alexander truly was: a king, a leader, and a conqueror destined to make history.

Alexander's triumph at Issus was more than just a win over Darius. It was a masterclass in strategy, bravery, and leadership. By outmaneuvering a larger army, capturing a king's family, and inspiring both his soldiers and his enemies, Alexander proved that he was no ordinary ruler. His journey was far from over, but with each battle, he moved closer to fulfilling his incredible dream of building an empire that would never be forgotten.

Questions

- How did the narrow plains of Issus give Alexander an advantage over the larger Persian army?

- What bold action did Alexander take to directly challenge King Darius III during the battle?

- What happened to King Darius' family after they were captured by Alexander's army?

- How did Alexander treat Darius' family, and why was this significant?

- Why was the Battle of Issus considered a turning point in Alexander's campaign against Persia?

The Siege of Tyre

Alexander the Great faced countless challenges on his journey to conquer the Persian Empire, but the city of Tyre would prove to be one of the toughest yet. Unlike other cities he had encountered, Tyre was an island fortress surrounded by water, making it nearly impossible to attack. It was strong, wealthy, and located in a spot that Alexander needed to control if he wanted to keep moving toward his goal.

Why Tyre Was So Important

Tyre wasn't just any city. It was a rich and powerful center of trade, where merchants brought goods from across the Mediterranean and beyond. More importantly, Tyre's location made it a strategic prize. If Alexander controlled Tyre, he could ensure that no Persian ships could use its harbors to challenge his growing empire.

But Tyre's leaders weren't ready to welcome Alexander with open arms. When Alexander sent a message asking them to surrender peacefully, they refused. They believed their city was untouchable because of its location on an island about half a mile from the coast. They had thick walls that towered over the sea, and their navy was ready to defend them.

For most armies, this would have been the end of the story. Conquering Tyre seemed impossible. But Alexander wasn't like most leaders. He saw challenges as puzzles to solve, and this puzzle was one he was determined to crack.

A Bold Plan

Alexander's first task was figuring out how to reach the island. Attacking by sea wasn't an option, as Tyre's navy controlled the waters. So, Alexander came up with an idea that seemed crazy at first: he would build a land bridge, or causeway, from the mainland to the island.

This was no small task. The waters between the coast and Tyre were deep and filled with slippery rocks. But Alexander's army got to work, piling stones, sand, and wood into the water to create a road that stretched toward the city. Day after day, the causeway grew longer, inching closer to Tyre.

The people of Tyre watched in disbelief. They hadn't expected Alexander to try something so bold. At first, they laughed, thinking it would never work. But as the causeway crept closer, their laughter turned to worry.

The Siege Begins

When the causeway neared the island, the people of Tyre fought back. They sent ships filled with flaming materials to burn the structure. They launched arrows and stones at Alexander's workers, making it difficult and dangerous to keep building.

But Alexander didn't give up. He protected his workers by building huge wooden towers on the causeway. These towers were covered with animal hides to shield them from fire and arrows, and they were armed with catapults that could hurl stones at Tyre's walls. With this protection, the workers continued their tasks.

At the same time, Alexander realized he couldn't rely on the causeway alone. He needed a navy to challenge Tyre's ships and blockade the city. So, he gathered ships from nearby allies and created a fleet strong enough to face Tyre's navy. With his army on land and his navy at sea, Alexander began a full-scale siege of the city.

Breaking Through

The siege lasted for months. Tyre's defenders were fierce and determined, but Alexander's persistence was even stronger. His navy attacked Tyre's harbors, cutting off supplies and weakening the city's defenses. Meanwhile, his army on the causeway built massive battering rams and siege towers to assault the city's walls.

Finally, after weeks of relentless attacks, Alexander's forces broke through. His soldiers stormed the city, climbing over its walls and fighting their way through the streets. The people of Tyre fought bravely, but they couldn't withstand Alexander's combined land and sea assault.

The Victory

The capture of Tyre was a monumental victory for Alexander. It showed the world that no city was beyond his reach, no matter how strong its defenses. Tyre had been a symbol of Persian power in the region, and now it was under Alexander's control.

But this victory wasn't just about strategy and strength. It also showed Alexander's incredible determination. He could have chosen to bypass Tyre and continue his campaign elsewhere, but he didn't. He saw the city's importance and refused to back down, even when the odds seemed impossible.

The Aftermath

After the fall of Tyre, Alexander's reputation as a brilliant and unstoppable leader grew even stronger. Cities across the region, hearing of Tyre's fate, began to surrender to him without a fight. They realized that resisting Alexander might lead to the same outcome as Tyre's—a long and costly defeat.

The causeway that Alexander built remained in place long after the battle, eventually connecting Tyre to the mainland permanently. Today, what was once an island is now part of the coast, a lasting reminder of Alexander's incredible siege.

The Siege of Tyre wasn't just a battle; it was a test of creativity, determination, and leadership. Alexander turned an impossible situation into a stunning victory by thinking outside the box and refusing to give up. His success at Tyre opened the door to even greater conquests, bringing him one step closer to his dream of uniting the known world under his rule.

Questions

- Why was Tyre such an important city for Alexander to conquer?
- What bold strategy did Alexander use to reach the island city of Tyre?
- How did the people of Tyre try to stop Alexander's causeway from reaching their city?
- What role did Alexander's navy play in the siege of Tyre?
- How did the capture of Tyre affect Alexander's reputation and future conquests?

Egypt and Founding Alexandria

After his stunning victory at Tyre, Alexander the Great turned his sights to Egypt. This land of golden deserts, mighty pyramids, and the legendary Nile River was unlike any place he had ever seen. Conquering Egypt would not only add another jewel to his growing empire but also bring him closer to defeating the mighty Persian Empire once and for all.

A Warm Welcome

When Alexander and his army arrived in Egypt, they were greeted with open arms. The Egyptians had long been under Persian rule and weren't exactly fans of their overlords. To them, Alexander wasn't just a conqueror—he was a liberator. The people welcomed him as a hero, offering food, gifts, and celebrations in his honor.

Unlike other lands Alexander had taken by force, Egypt didn't require a single battle. This was a refreshing change for the young king and his tired soldiers. For the first time in months, they could rest without the constant fear of war.

A Journey to the Oracle of Siwa

Alexander wasn't the type to sit still for long. While his men enjoyed the comforts of Egypt, Alexander set off on a mysterious journey deep into the desert. His destination? The Oracle of Siwa was an ancient and revered temple believed to hold answers to life's greatest questions.

Why would Alexander trek across scorching sands to visit this remote shrine? The Oracle was said to offer wisdom and guidance through its priests, who were thought to possess remarkable insight. People from far and wide visited Siwa, seeking clarity and direction.

The journey was anything but easy. Alexander and his small group of companions faced blinding sandstorms and scorching heat. Yet, the challenge only fueled his determination. According to legend, when the travelers were on the verge of losing their way, two snakes—or perhaps two crows—appeared to guide them safely to the temple.

When Alexander finally arrived, the priests welcomed him warmly. Inside the sacred temple, they performed ancient rituals and declared something extraordinary: Alexander was destined for greatness. Whether this was based on their traditions or simply a gesture of respect, the declaration had a profound impact.

This moment further solidified Alexander's confidence and position as a leader who believed in his destiny to rule. Whether people saw it as a spiritual truth or a symbolic gesture, what truly mattered was the influence it had on his followers and the legacy he was building.

Founding Alexandria

Inspired by his experience at the Oracle, Alexander returned to the Egyptian coast with a grand vision. He decided to build a city that would stand as a symbol of his power and ambition. This city would be named Alexandria, after himself, and would become a shining beacon of culture and learning for centuries to come.

Alexander chose a spot near the Mediterranean Sea, where the Nile River branched into a lush delta. The location was perfect for trade, with easy access to both the river and the sea. He personally helped design the city, laying out wide streets, grand buildings, and a massive harbor.

One of the most impressive features of Alexandria was its lighthouse, the Pharos of Alexandria. Though it wasn't completed during Alexander's lifetime, the lighthouse would eventually become one of the Seven Wonders of the Ancient World. Towering above the harbor, it guided ships safely to shore and became a symbol of the city's importance.

But Alexandria wasn't just about trade and architecture. Alexander dreamed of creating a place where people from different cultures could come together. Over the years, the city became a hub of art, science, and philosophy. Scholars from all over the ancient world flocked to its famous library, which housed hundreds of thousands of scrolls.

Winning Hearts and Minds

Alexander's time in Egypt wasn't just about building cities and consulting oracles. He also knew the importance of winning the hearts of the people. Rather than forcing Egyptian traditions to change, he respected them. He showed respect for their beliefs, honored their traditions, and even adopted some of their customs.

This strategy worked brilliantly. The Egyptians saw Alexander as a leader who understood their culture, not as a foreign invader. This respect helped secure their loyalty and made Egypt a stable part of his growing empire.

Looking Ahead

By the time Alexander left Egypt, he had accomplished more than most kings could dream of in a lifetime. He had been hailed as a liberator and founded a city that would become one of the greatest in history. Yet, for Alexander, this was just the beginning.

His sights were set on an even bigger prize: the heart of the Persian Empire. With Egypt now under his control, Alexander could march forward with confidence, knowing his rear was secure.

Alexander's time in Egypt showed not just his military brilliance but also his ability to inspire and connect with people from different cultures. His vision for Alexandria reflected his belief in the power of knowledge and unity, ideas that would leave a lasting legacy long after his time. As he prepared to face new challenges, Alexander carried with him the lessons and victories he had gained in this land of pharaohs and pyramids.

Questions

- Why did the Egyptians welcome Alexander so warmly when he arrived in their land?

- What made the journey to the Oracle of Siwa so challenging for Alexander and his companions?

- What was Alexander's vision for the city of Alexandria, and why did he choose its specific location?

- How did Alexander show respect for Egyptian traditions during his time there?

- What was the significance of the Pharos of Alexandria, and why was it considered a wonder of the ancient world?

The Battle of Gaugamela

Alexander the Great had faced many challenges in his quest to conquer the Persian Empire, but he knew the greatest test was still ahead. King Darius III, ruler of Persia, was not about to give up his empire without a fight. He had assembled a massive army at a place called Gaugamela, determined to stop Alexander once and for all. But Alexander wasn't afraid. Instead, he saw this as his chance to win it all and become the ruler of Asia.

Preparing for Greatness

Before the battle, Alexander spent weeks preparing his army. He wasn't just focused on sharpening swords and polishing shields—

he was planning a strategy that would give him the upper hand, even against an army much larger than his own.

Darius had gathered troops from all corners of his vast empire. Some estimates say his army was five times the size of Alexander's! But Alexander knew that victory didn't just depend on numbers—it depended on clever tactics and the loyalty of his men.

Alexander studied the battlefield carefully. Gaugamela was a flat plain, perfect for Darius's massive army and his war chariots, which had razor-sharp blades attached to their wheels. But Alexander wasn't worried. He was a master of using the land to his advantage, and he had a plan.

A Battle for the Ages

The night before the battle, Alexander's troops rested while Darius's army stayed awake, anxious and preparing for the fight.

When the sun rose, the stage was set for one of the most famous battles in history.

Darius had positioned his forces to make the most of his numbers. He placed his chariots at the front and his strongest warriors at the center. His plan was to overwhelm Alexander with sheer force. But Alexander had a different idea.

As the battle began, Alexander ordered his troops to move diagonally, pulling Darius's forces toward one side. This created an opening in the Persian line—a weak spot Alexander had been waiting for. At the same time, his cavalry (soldiers on horseback) struck with lightning speed, keeping the Persians off balance.

Darius unleashed his war chariots, hoping to crush Alexander's soldiers. But Alexander's men were ready. They used their spears to take down the horses and even let some chariots pass through their ranks, creating traps to stop them.

Then, Alexander made his boldest move. He led a charge straight at Darius's center, aiming for the king himself. The sight of Alexander charging with his soldiers was so terrifying that many Persian warriors panicked and fled.

Darius, seeing his forces crumble, turned his chariot around and ran from the battlefield. With their king gone, the Persian army fell apart.

A Legendary Victory

The victory at Gaugamela wasn't just a win for Alexander—it was the turning point of his entire campaign. By defeating Darius's massive army, Alexander had effectively conquered the Persian Empire. Cities and regions that once belonged to Darius now pledged their loyalty to Alexander.

After the battle, Alexander entered Babylon, one of the most magnificent cities of the ancient world. The people welcomed him as their new ruler, offering gifts and celebrating his arrival. He treated them with respect, just as he had done in Egypt, and began to take on the role of a true king, not just a conqueror.

But what about Darius? The Persian king fled east, hoping to gather another army and take back his empire. Alexander pursued him relentlessly, determined to end the Persian threat once and for all.

The Fall of the Persian Empire

Darius didn't get far. His own generals betrayed him, and he was eventually killed. When Alexander found his body, he was furious—not because Darius was his enemy, but because he believed kings should be treated with honor, even in defeat. Alexander gave Darius a proper burial and declared himself the rightful ruler of the Persian Empire.

With Darius gone, Alexander was now the most powerful man in the world. He had achieved what many thought was impossible: the complete overthrow of the Persian Empire. But Alexander wasn't done. He saw himself not just as a conqueror but as a unifier. He wanted to blend Greek and Persian cultures, creating a new world where people of different backgrounds could live together.

Why Gaugamela Mattered

The Battle of Gaugamela wasn't just another fight—it was a moment that changed history. Alexander's clever tactics showed that brains could beat brawn, and his leadership inspired loyalty and bravery in his men. Even though they were outnumbered, they fought with everything they had because they believed in their leader.

The victory also cemented Alexander's reputation as one of the greatest military commanders of all time. Stories of his bravery and intelligence spread far and wide, making him a legend in his own lifetime.

Moving Forward

With the Persian Empire under his control, Alexander's empire stretched from Greece to Egypt to Asia. But for Alexander, there were always more lands to explore and conquer. He wasn't content to rest on his achievements—he wanted to push the boundaries of the known world.

Yet, even as he dreamed of future conquests, Alexander knew the victory at Gaugamela would always stand out. It wasn't just the battle that made him ruler of Asia—it was the moment that proved anything was possible with courage, determination, and a brilliant plan.

The Battle of Gaugamela was more than just a fight between two armies. It was a clash of strategies, a test of leadership, and a turning point in Alexander's incredible journey. Against all odds, Alexander had triumphed, showing the world what true greatness looked like. As his empire grew, so did his vision for what it could become—a vision that started with one legendary battle on the plains of Gaugamela.

Questions

- Why did King Darius III choose Gaugamela as the battlefield for his massive army?

- What clever tactic did Alexander use to create a weak spot in the Persian line?

- How did Alexander's troops handle Darius's war chariots during the battle?

- What happened to King Darius III after his defeat at Gaugamela?

- Why is the Battle of Gaugamela considered a turning point in Alexander's conquest?

The Fall of Persepolis

Alexander the Great had done it again. After defeating King Darius III at the Battle of Gaugamela, he pushed further into Persia. But this wasn't just about winning battles anymore. Alexander wanted to take control of Persia's greatest treasures, prove his authority as a ruler, and unite two worlds—Greece and Persia. His journey now led him to the heart of the Persian Empire: the legendary city of Persepolis.

The Jewel of Persia

Persepolis was like no other city Alexander had ever seen. Built by the Persian kings to show off their power and wealth, it was filled with grand palaces, towering columns, and breathtaking statues. Gold and silver sparkled everywhere, from the walls to the floors. For centuries, Persepolis had been the center of Persian culture and power, but now it stood before Alexander as a prize waiting to be claimed.

When Alexander and his army marched into Persepolis, they were awestruck by its beauty. But they also knew what it symbolized. Persepolis wasn't just a city—it was a symbol of Persian pride and strength. By taking it, Alexander was sending a clear message to the world: the Persian Empire was no more, and he was its new ruler.

Treasure Fit for a King

One of the first things Alexander did in Persepolis was explore its incredible treasures. The city was home to unimaginable riches—golden statues, jeweled thrones, and mountains of coins. Historians say that the treasure Alexander took from Persepolis was so vast that it took thousands of men and animals months to carry it all away.

But Alexander didn't keep all this wealth for himself. He used it to reward his soldiers, fund his future campaigns, and strengthen his growing empire. To him, these treasures weren't just shiny objects—they were tools to build something greater.

The Night the Flames Rose

Not long after taking Persepolis, something happened that would be talked about for centuries. One night, a grand banquet was held in the city, filled with food, music, and laughter. As the celebration went on, Alexander made a decision that shocked even his closest friends: he ordered Persepolis to be set on fire.

Why would Alexander burn such a magnificent city? Some say it was an act of revenge for how the Persians had burned Athens years earlier. Others believe it was a decision made in the heat of the moment.

Whatever the reason, the flames consumed the palaces and halls, reducing much of Persepolis to ruins. The fire wasn't just about destroying a city—it was a powerful symbol. It marked the end of the Persian Empire and the beginning of something new. But for Alexander, it was also a turning point. After the fire, he began to see himself not just as a conqueror but as a ruler with a greater mission.

A King of Two Worlds

Up until now, Alexander had been a Macedonian king leading a Greek army. But with the fall of Persepolis, he ruled over both Greeks and Persians, two very different cultures. Instead of treating the Persians as enemies, Alexander wanted to bring them into his empire.

He began adopting Persian customs, wearing their clothes, and even surrounding himself with Persian advisors. Some of his Greek followers didn't like this—they thought he was abandoning his roots. But Alexander saw it differently. He wasn't just the king of Greece or Persia anymore. He was the king of a vast empire, and he wanted to unite the people under his rule.

To show his commitment, Alexander encouraged his soldiers to marry Persian women, blending the two cultures. He believed that by bringing Greeks and Persians together, he could create a new, stronger world.

Leadership and Legacy

Alexander's time in Persepolis also changed how he saw himself as a leader. He wasn't just a warrior charging into battle—he was a ruler responsible for millions of people. He began to focus more on governing, organizing his empire, and planning for the future.

But this new role wasn't without its challenges. Some of his old friends and generals started questioning his decisions, especially his embrace of Persian customs. They worried that he was drifting too far from the man they had followed into battle.

Despite this, Alexander stayed firm in his vision. He believed that by blending the best of Greek and Persian cultures, he could create something truly extraordinary. And while not everyone agreed with his methods, they couldn't deny his determination and charisma.

The Road Ahead

With Persepolis behind him, Alexander's journey was far from over. He set his sights even further east, toward the edges of the known world. However, the capture of

Persepolis and his transformation into a king of both Greeks and Persians marked a turning point in his story.

Alexander was no longer just a conqueror. He was a builder, a visionary, and a ruler who dreamed of uniting people from different lands and backgrounds.

The capture of Persepolis and the events that followed showed the world a different side of Alexander. He wasn't just a military genius—he was a leader who saw the bigger picture. By taking the treasures of Persia, burning the city, and embracing its culture, Alexander laid the foundation for a new kind of empire, one that blended the best of two worlds. His journey was far from over, but in Persepolis, he had taken a giant step toward achieving his ultimate goals.

Questions

- Why was Persepolis considered an important city in the Persian Empire?
- What did Alexander do with the vast treasures he found in Persepolis?
- What event led to the destruction of much of Persepolis?
- How did Alexander begin to unite Greek and Persian cultures after capturing Persepolis?
- Why did some of Alexander's Greek followers question his decisions after the fall of Persepolis?

Journey into Central Asia

After Alexander's stunning victories in Persia, he wasn't ready to stop. His journey now led him to the wild lands of Central Asia. These were places called Bactria and Sogdiana, areas that were far from the familiar lands he had conquered before. These regions were tough and mysterious—full of high mountains, vast deserts, and cities surrounded by thick walls. Alexander's army would face many new challenges, but they were also about to make history in ways they never expected.

Into the Wilds of Bactria and Sogdiana

The march into Bactria and Sogdiana was one of Alexander's most difficult. The land was rough, with mountains so tall that it felt like they reached the sky. In the beginning, Alexander's army was confident. They were used to facing challenges and had already won battles in many different places. But these regions tested them in new ways. The people in Bactria and Sogdiana were not easily defeated. They were fierce warriors who lived in mountain fortresses, and many of their cities were surrounded by thick walls that made it hard to attack.

One of the first big challenges Alexander and his army faced was the city of Bactra. The city was well-protected, with strong walls and well-trained soldiers. But Alexander wasn't the kind of leader who gave up easily. He used his clever strategies to outsmart the defenders. By surrounding the city and cutting off their supplies, Alexander forced them to surrender. But this victory was just the beginning. As Alexander moved deeper into Central Asia, he found that the people of Bactria and Sogdiana were willing to fight for their freedom.

The Great Marriage of Roxana

In the middle of all the battles and conquests, Alexander made an important decision that would change the future of his empire. He married a princess named Roxana, who came from the region of Bactria. Why did he do this? Well, marrying Roxana was more than just about a wedding—it was a smart political move.

By marrying a local princess, Alexander hoped to unite the Greek and Central Asian cultures. He wanted the people of Bactria and Sogdiana to feel like they were part of his empire. This marriage showed that he wasn't just a conqueror from Greece—he was now a ruler who understood the importance of blending different cultures. In fact, Alexander believed that combining the best of both cultures could make his empire even stronger.

Alexander's decision to marry Roxana wasn't just about making peace. It was a move that symbolized unity. By marrying her, he tied his fate to the people of the land he was trying to rule. Roxana's family became important allies, and her marriage to Alexander helped to bring the people of Central Asia closer to his empire.

Tough Marches and Even Tougher Battles

As Alexander's army continued its journey, they faced many obstacles. The land was rough and unfamiliar. Sometimes, the army would march for days through deserts, only to face freezing nights in the mountains. It wasn't just the terrain that was difficult, but the weather, too. One day, they would be walking through a burning hot desert, and the next, they would be stuck in the snow, trying to keep warm. These conditions tested Alexander's soldiers, but they pushed on.

Besides the weather and the difficult landscape, Alexander and his army had to deal with local rebellions. Not everyone was happy to have a foreign ruler. In many places, the people didn't want to be ruled by someone from Greece, even though Alexander tried to bring peace through his clever marriage to Roxana. Many of the cities in Bactria and Sogdiana put up fierce resistance, and Alexander had to lead his army through some of the toughest battles of his career. The people of the region had a strong will to defend their land, and Alexander knew he had to keep pushing forward if he was going to make his empire strong.

Victory Through Persistence

Even though the marches were long and tiring, Alexander's army didn't back down.

Through careful planning and relentless effort, they conquered the tough mountain cities one by one. But it wasn't just his soldiers who made the difference—it was Alexander's sharp mind. He studied the land, used the terrain to his advantage, and came up with creative ways to overcome the challenges they faced.

At one point, Alexander even led his soldiers up a steep mountain to defeat a strong enemy force. His soldiers were exhausted, but Alexander encouraged them to keep going, showing them that their determination could turn any battle in their favor. The journey was difficult, but every victory made the army more powerful and more determined to succeed.

Building Strong Bonds

During this part of his journey, Alexander also started to change how he ruled. He didn't just rely on his Greek soldiers anymore; he began to recruit local men into his army. He saw the value in learning from the people who lived in these lands, and he knew that by bringing them into his army, he could build a stronger, more united force. This was another way Alexander showed that he was not just a conqueror—he was a ruler who understood the importance of cooperation.

While many of his Greek soldiers weren't thrilled about the idea of fighting alongside local soldiers, Alexander's leadership skills helped him convince them. He made sure his men knew that these alliances were key to building a lasting empire. He encouraged his army to respect the local cultures they encountered, and they began to form connections with the people they met.

The journey into Central Asia was one of the most challenging parts of Alexander's campaign. He faced new enemies, harsh weather, and difficult terrain, but he also showed the world that he could lead through persistence and intelligence. His marriage to Roxana was an important step in uniting different cultures and proving that Alexander was more than just a conqueror—he was a ruler who sought peace and unity.

Through these campaigns, Alexander proved that no matter how tough the journey, a true leader never gives up. His journey into Central Asia was just one of many steps in his quest to create an empire that would stretch across the known world. Though the challenges were great, Alexander and his army pushed forward, always striving for victory. And with every step, they built a future that would be remembered for centuries.

Questions

- What was the strategic reason behind Alexander's marriage to Roxana?

- How did Alexander's army overcome the challenges of rough terrain and weather in Central Asia?

- What role did Alexander's clever leadership play in the conquest of Bactria and Sogdiana?

- How did Alexander encourage his soldiers to work with the local people of Central Asia?

- Why was Alexander's journey into Central Asia a significant part of his campaign?

Crossing the Hindu Kush

It was the year 327 BCE, and Alexander the Great was about to face one of the most challenging parts of his journey. After conquering Persia and many lands to the west, Alexander's army was now pushing forward to invade India. But first, they had to cross the mighty Hindu Kush mountains—a range so tall and treacherous it felt like nature itself was testing their willpower.

The Hindu Kush mountains were located in what is now Afghanistan. They stood as huge, jagged peaks that stretched high into the sky. To get to India, Alexander knew they would have to go through these mountains. The army wasn't just facing mountains, though. They also had to deal with freezing cold, snowstorms, and the dangerous tribes who lived in the area. It was going to be a tough journey.

Battling the Elements

As the army began to make its way toward the Hindu Kush, the weather turned cold and bitter. One of the hardest things to deal with was the freezing temperature. Soldiers who were used to the warmth of Persia or the Mediterranean now had to march through snow and ice, with their feet sometimes sinking into deep drifts. The air became thin, and it was hard to breathe as they climbed higher into the mountains.

The weather was so harsh that even the horses had trouble moving. Some soldiers lost their strength and could barely keep going. The cold, the snow, and the steep cliffs made it hard to move quickly. But Alexander, as usual, wasn't about to back down. He led by example, encouraging his soldiers to push on. Even though many were exhausted, they knew that they had to keep moving. There was no turning back.

Fighting Fierce Tribes

The journey through the Hindu Kush wasn't just about the weather and the tough terrain. Along the way, Alexander's army had to face fierce tribes that lived in the mountains. These tribes weren't afraid to fight. In fact, they had been living in these rugged lands for centuries, and they were expert fighters. They knew the terrain better than anyone, which made it even harder for Alexander's army to get through.

One of the most important battles took place with the tribe of the Mallian people. The Mallians lived in a stronghold that was located in a high, fortified city. Their warriors were tough, and they weren't going to let Alexander pass through without a fight.

But Alexander had a plan. He used his usual strategy of clever tactics and military skill. Instead of charging straight at the city, he surrounded it, using his army to set up a blockade. He cut off any way for the Mallians to escape or get help from nearby tribes. After a fierce battle, Alexander's army was able to break through the defenses, forcing the Mallians to surrender. This victory gave Alexander control over more key routes through the Hindu Kush and helped him prepare for what lay ahead in India.

Securing Key Routes

One of Alexander's greatest skills was his ability to recognize the importance of securing key routes and locations. As his army moved through the Hindu Kush, it wasn't just about fighting battles—it was about making sure they had safe passage through the mountains. If Alexander and his men couldn't find a way through the mountains, their entire mission would be in danger.

Alexander knew that the roads through the Hindu Kush would lead him to India, where he planned to conquer even more lands. In order to do this, he had to make sure he had a safe way to get through the mountains. Securing key points along the way, like towns and passes, allowed Alexander to move his army without fear of attack.

The soldiers worked hard to clear paths, build roads, and create camps along the way. Every little victory helped them get closer to their ultimate goal—India. The army's perseverance in these tough conditions showed how determined they were to achieve Alexander's dream of reaching the land of the Indus River.

Preparing for India

After many weeks of fighting battles, surviving the harsh weather, and clearing the dangerous paths of the Hindu Kush, Alexander and his army finally reached the border of India. They were exhausted, but they had made it through the mountains. And now, the Indian subcontinent lay in front of them—a land full of mysteries, new cultures, and new challenges.

But before they could march into India, Alexander knew that his army needed time to rest and regroup. They had been on the road for a long time, and they had been through a lot. The soldiers had to recover their strength, prepare for the new battles ahead, and get ready for the unknown challenges of India.

The men were eager to face their next challenge, but some of them were also worried. Many of the soldiers had heard stories about the powerful Indian armies and the lands they would face. It wasn't going to be easy, and the soldiers knew that they would need to be stronger than ever to continue their journey.

Despite their concerns, Alexander wasn't worried. He had always found a way to overcome obstacles before, and he was confident that his army would be able to conquer whatever stood in their way. As the days passed, the soldiers trained, rested, and got ready for their march into India.

A Legend in the Making

Crossing the Hindu Kush and preparing for the invasion of India wasn't just a difficult challenge—it was a key part of Alexander's story. It showed how far he was willing to go to achieve his dreams. No matter how tough things got, Alexander didn't give up. He led his men through some of the most challenging conditions imaginable, and each victory made him stronger and more determined to succeed.

By the time Alexander's army was ready to march into India, they had already accomplished so much. They had conquered lands from Greece all the way to the edge of Central Asia. They had battled fierce tribes, survived freezing cold temperatures, and fought their way through difficult mountain passes. The army's grit and determination had brought them this far, and they were ready for whatever lay ahead.

In many ways, the journey through the Hindu Kush was one of the most important parts of Alexander's campaign. It showed that no matter how difficult the road was, he would always find a way to push through. And with that attitude, he would go on to achieve some of the greatest victories the world had ever seen. The journey to India was just the beginning of the next chapter in Alexander's incredible story.

Questions

- What made crossing the Hindu Kush mountains so difficult for Alexander's army?
- Which tribe did Alexander's army fight during their journey through the Hindu Kush?
- How did Alexander secure safe passage through the Hindu Kush?
- Why did Alexander's army need to rest and prepare before continuing into India?
- What were some of the challenges Alexander faced before his invasion of India?

The Battle of the Hydaspes River

The sun blazed down on the dusty land as Alexander and his army moved forward, their eyes focused on the horizon. They had crossed countless lands, faced powerful armies, and won many battles. But now, they were about to meet an enemy that would test their strength and courage in a way they hadn't experienced before. This time, it wasn't just any enemy—this was King Porus of India, and he had something very special in his army: war elephants.

The Battle of the Hydaspes River was about to begin, and it would change Alexander's journey forever.

The Challenge of the River

The first challenge Alexander faced was the mighty Hydaspes River. It was wide and deep, its waters flowing fast and strong. Alexander needed to cross it, but it wasn't easy. On the other side of the river, King Porus waited with his huge army. They had the advantage of being on higher ground, ready to defend the riverbanks.

But Alexander wasn't worried. He knew that to win, he had to be smart. He spent days studying the river and the land around it. His soldiers worked together to build boats, and soon, they were ready to cross.

One night, while Porus was resting, Alexander decided it was time to act. He led his soldiers across the river at a point where the enemy didn't expect. They crossed in the dark, moving quickly and quietly, and by morning, Alexander's army was on the other side. Porus was shocked when he realized that the Macedonian army had crossed the river without him knowing!

The Mighty War Elephants

As Alexander and his army faced King Porus's forces, they saw something they had never seen before: massive war elephants. These elephants were huge, strong, and covered in armor. They were like walking tanks, carrying soldiers on their backs. The sight of them made the Macedonian soldiers nervous. They had never fought against such creatures before, and it seemed impossible to defeat them.

But Alexander was not the kind of leader to back down from a challenge. He quickly realized that these elephants were both a strength and a weakness. They were powerful, but they needed space to move around. If Alexander could stop them from moving freely, he could defeat Porus's army.

A Brilliant Plan

Alexander had always been a brilliant strategist, and this battle would be no different. He quickly came up with a clever plan. He decided to split his army into smaller groups and attack from different directions. This would confuse Porus's army and force them to spread out, giving Alexander the chance to use his best soldiers to target the war elephants.

As the battle began, Alexander's cavalry moved quickly and silently, hitting the enemy from the sides. At the same time, his archers fired arrows at the elephants, aiming for their eyes and legs. The elephants, confused and hurt, started to panic. The soldiers on the elephants tried to control them, but it was difficult. The chaos caused by Alexander's attack made it hard for Porus to organize his forces.

Meanwhile, Alexander led his infantry forward, charging at the heart of Porus's army. His soldiers fought with all their might, and the battle became a wild, chaotic struggle. The Macedonians were fierce and well-trained, while the Indian soldiers were brave and determined.

Turning the Tide

Despite the odds, Alexander's plan worked. Slowly but surely, the Macedonians gained the upper hand. The elephants, once the key to Porus's army, were no longer a threat. Without them, the Indian soldiers were thrown into disarray. Porus's forces started to retreat, and the Macedonians pressed forward.

After hours of fighting, it was clear that Alexander had won. Porus, however, was not easily defeated. He fought with great courage, refusing to give up. When Alexander saw that the battle was over, he sent a message to King Porus. He asked him to come and speak face to face.

A Respectful Rivalry

When Porus arrived, injured but proud, Alexander showed him great respect. He was impressed by Porus's bravery and leadership. Instead of humiliating him, Alexander decided to treat him as an equal. "How do you wish to be treated?" Alexander asked the defeated king.

Porus replied, "Like a king."

Alexander, showing kindness and respect, agreed. He not only spared Porus's life but also gave him back his kingdom. He even offered him soldiers to help defend his land from any future threats. The two men, once enemies on the battlefield, formed a friendship based on mutual respect. Alexander admired Porus's strength and courage, and Porus admired Alexander's tactics and leadership.

The Victory and the Future

The Battle of the Hydaspes River was a turning point for Alexander. Not only had he defeated a powerful army, but he had also proven that he could outsmart even the most difficult challenges. With Porus's army defeated, Alexander's path into India was now open.

After the battle, Alexander continued his campaign, pushing further into India. But the Hydaspes battle remained one of his most famous victories, remembered for the clever tactics he used to overcome a much larger and more powerful force. It also marked the moment when Alexander showed that he was not just a conqueror but a leader who could earn the respect of his enemies.

Though Alexander's soldiers were tired and longing to return home, the Macedonian king's ambition burned brightly. He dreamed of new lands, new victories, and even greater challenges ahead. But the Battle of the Hydaspes had taught him something important: even the most powerful army could be defeated with the right plan, and even the toughest enemies could become friends.

In the end, Alexander's victory at the Hydaspes River wasn't just about winning a battle. It was about proving that with determination, respect, and brilliant tactics, anything was possible. And as the dust settled on the battlefield, Alexander's legend continued to grow—one battle at a time.

Questions

- What made the Hydaspes River a challenging obstacle for Alexander and his army to cross?
- How did Alexander manage to confuse King Porus's forces during the battle?
- Why were the war elephants both an advantage and a disadvantage for Porus's army?
- What was Alexander's reaction when he finally met King Porus after the battle?
- How did Alexander show respect for King Porus after winning the Battle of the Hydaspes River?

The Limits of Conquest

Alexander the Great stood at the edge of a dream. He had crossed mountains, battled fierce armies, and faced challenges that would have stopped anyone else. But here he was, staring into the vast lands of India. It was a place of mystery, riches, and stories about even greater kingdoms farther away. Alexander was ready for more. His soldiers, however, had a very different idea.

For years, his army had marched with him across deserts, rivers, and mountains. They had followed him into battle after battle, and they had won them all. But they were tired—more tired than Alexander could imagine. They missed their homes, their families, and the familiar comforts of

Macedonia and Greece. The lush lands of India might have tempted Alexander, but for his soldiers, it felt like the world was pulling them too far from everything they loved.

One day, as Alexander prepared to share his grand plans to march deeper into India, the murmurs in the camp grew louder. Soldiers whispered to each other, their faces filled with exhaustion. They weren't just tired in their bodies; they were tired in their hearts. And then it happened. A brave soldier stepped forward to speak on behalf of them all.

"Alexander," the soldier said, bowing slightly but speaking firmly, "we have followed you across the world. We've stood beside you in every battle. But now, we ask you to listen to us. We've gone far enough. Let us go home."

Alexander was stunned. His army had never refused him before. He looked around at the men who had fought so bravely for him. Their armor was scratched and dented from countless battles. Their faces showed courage but also longing—a deep desire to see the places they had left behind.

At first, Alexander tried to persuade them. He spoke of the glory that awaited them if they conquered the lands ahead. He promised riches and stories that would make them legends. But his words didn't ignite the usual fire in their eyes. The soldiers remained silent, standing firm like a mountain that couldn't be moved.

Finally, Alexander realized that pushing them further would break their spirits. These men weren't just his soldiers—they were his companions, the ones who had made his conquests possible. With a heavy heart, he made the decision to turn back.

The Journey Home

The decision to retreat didn't mean the journey would be easy. Far from it. Alexander now had to lead his army back through lands that weren't always friendly. Rivers had to be crossed, deserts had to be traversed, and food had to be found for thousands of men and their animals.

One of the hardest parts of the retreat was crossing the Gedrosian Desert. The heat was unbearable, and the sand seemed to stretch forever. Water was scarce, and the soldiers struggled to keep going. But Alexander didn't just command from the front—he marched alongside his men, sharing in their hardships.

One day, a small group of soldiers found a bit of water in a dry, cracked streambed. They scooped it up in a helmet and brought it to Alexander. The men were parched, but they offered the water to their leader first.

Alexander looked at the helmet of water, then at his soldiers, who were watching him with sunburned faces and dry, cracked lips.

Without saying a word, Alexander poured the water onto the ground. The soldiers gasped, but then they understood. Alexander was showing them that if they couldn't drink, he wouldn't drink either. That moment filled the men with a new determination to keep going, even as the desert tested their limits.

Building Bridges, Not Just Empires

As they made their way back, Alexander didn't just focus on survival. He thought about how to leave a positive mark on the lands they had passed through. In many places, he stopped to build relationships with the local people.

In one town, Alexander met a group of elders who were worried about what would happen after his army left. Instead of taking their concerns lightly, Alexander listened. He worked with them to establish fair leaders who would maintain peace. He also left behind some of his men to help share ideas and cultures, blending the ways of the Greeks with the customs of the locals.

One of Alexander's greatest strengths was his ability to inspire loyalty, even among those he had once fought. He treated former enemies with respect and often invited them to join him as allies. This approach didn't just make him a conqueror—it made him a unifier, someone who brought people together instead of driving them apart.

A Leader Like No Other

By the time Alexander and his army reached safer lands, they had grown stronger as a group despite the hardships. The journey back wasn't just about retreating; it was about learning, growing, and finding new ways to connect with the world.

Alexander never saw himself as just a warrior. He dreamed of a world where different cultures could share knowledge and ideas. That's why he encouraged his men to marry women from the lands they had conquered, as he had married Roxana. He believed that by joining families and cultures, they could build a more unified and peaceful world.

Though not everyone agreed with Alexander's vision, there was no denying his ability to dream big. His soldiers may have been ready to stop marching, but they still respected the leader who had taken them farther than anyone had ever gone before.

Looking Ahead

As Alexander's army finally began to approach familiar territories, the soldiers felt a mixture of relief and pride. They had faced some of the toughest challenges imaginable, but they had survived. Alexander, too, felt a sense of accomplishment, though he couldn't help but think about the dreams he had left unfinished.

For Alexander, the retreat wasn't the end of his story—it was just another chapter in a life filled with incredible adventures. He had shown the world what was possible when courage, determination, and a touch of genius came together. And even as the army marched toward home, Alexander's mind was already spinning with new ideas and possibilities.

Who knew what lay ahead for the young king who had dared to dream so big? One thing was certain: wherever Alexander went, history followed. And even the toughest challenges couldn't dim the light of his ambition.

Questions

- Why did Alexander's soldiers refuse to continue marching further into India?

- What did Alexander do with the helmet of water in the Gedrosian Desert, and why?

- How did Alexander work to build relationships with the local people during the retreat?

- What was one of the biggest challenges Alexander and his army faced while crossing the Gedrosian Desert?

- How did Alexander try to unite different cultures as they journeyed back home?

The Return to Babylon

Alexander and his army were finally heading back home, but the journey wasn't a straight line or an easy one. They had to cross one of the most unforgiving places on Earth—the Gedrosian Desert. This stretch of land was hot, dry, and full of dangers. For Alexander, it was another test of his determination and his leadership.

Into the Desert

The Gedrosian Desert wasn't like anything most of the soldiers had ever seen. It was endless sand, blazing heat, and little to no water. The sun beat down so hard that even the bravest warriors struggled to keep going. Food and water were scarce, and many animals pulling the carts collapsed from exhaustion.

Alexander had hoped to follow this route to show his men—and the world—that he could conquer even nature. But the desert wasn't an enemy you could defeat with a sword or clever tactics.

Losses Along the Way

The desert didn't just test their spirits. It took a heavy toll. Many soldiers and animals didn't make it. Supplies were lost in sandstorms, and hunger gnawed at everyone. Alexander saw how hard it was on his people, but he never gave up. He walked alongside them, sharing their pain and refusing any special treatment.

Even with all the hardships, Alexander's

leadership held the army together. His ability to inspire his men, even in the toughest moments, showed why they followed him into impossible situations.

Finally Reaching Civilization

After what felt like an eternity, the army finally emerged from the desert. The relief was incredible. They reached towns where they could eat, drink, and rest. For the first time in weeks, they felt human again. The survivors looked back on the desert crossing as one of the hardest challenges of their lives.

Back to Babylon

In 324 BCE, Alexander and his army returned to Babylon, the city he had claimed years before. It was a grand, bustling place full of life and activity. For Alexander,

Babylon wasn't just another city—it was the heart of his growing empire.

But Alexander's work was far from over. While the desert journey was behind him, he now had to focus on something just as challenging: reorganizing his vast empire.

Fixing What Was Broken

Alexander's empire stretched from Greece to Egypt to India. It was enormous, and keeping it all running smoothly was no small task. While he had been out conquering new lands, problems had popped up in different regions. Some governors had grown too powerful, and others were accused of mistreating the people.

Alexander didn't waste time. He investigated the complaints, removed corrupt leaders, and replaced them with people he trusted. He wanted his empire to be strong and fair, with everyone working together.

Blending Cultures

One of Alexander's biggest goals was to bring different cultures together. He believed that his empire would be stronger if people from different lands saw each other as allies instead of enemies. To make this happen, he encouraged marriages between his soldiers and women from the regions they had conquered.

Alexander himself had already married Roxana from Central Asia, and now he organized a massive wedding event where thousands of his men married women from Persia. It was his way of showing that Greeks, Persians, and others could live and work together as one people.

Celebrations and Planning

Back in Babylon, the city buzzed with activity. Alexander held grand feasts to celebrate the victories and survival of his army. He rewarded his soldiers for their loyalty and bravery, giving them gold and treasures from his conquests.

But Alexander wasn't just celebrating. He was also planning. He wanted to keep expanding his empire, with dreams of exploring Arabia and other lands. He imagined cities, roads, and new trade routes that would connect his empire like never before.

A Leader's Reflection

Though Alexander was only in his early 30s, he had achieved more than most people could dream of in a lifetime. He had built one of the largest empires the world had ever seen, and his name was known far and wide. But he wasn't someone who sat back and relaxed. He was always thinking about what came next.

Still, there were moments in Babylon when he would sit quietly and look out over the city. The Euphrates River flowed gently through it, and the streets were alive with merchants, farmers, and families. Perhaps Alexander wondered about the cost of his conquests—the lives lost and the challenges ahead.

Preparing for the Future

Even as Alexander worked to strengthen his empire, some people whispered about what might happen if he were no longer in charge. His generals were loyal to him, but they were ambitious, too. Who would rule such a vast empire if Alexander wasn't around?

Alexander didn't have a clear answer. His focus was on building, conquering, and uniting, not on what might happen if he wasn't there to lead. For now, he was determined to keep moving forward, no matter the challenges.

The Legacy of Babylon

Alexander's time in Babylon marked an important chapter in his life. It was a moment of triumph, reflection, and planning. The city became a symbol of his vision for a united empire where people from different cultures could work together.

But even as Alexander reorganized his empire and celebrated with his people, the challenges of ruling such a vast and diverse land were just beginning. There were still many roads to travel, and Alexander, ever the dreamer and leader, was ready to face them head-on.

Babylon, with its towering walls and vibrant streets, would always hold a special place in Alexander's story. It was where he showed that being a great leader wasn't just about winning battles—it was also about bringing people together and building a future for everyone.

Questions

- What challenges did Alexander and his army face while crossing the Gedrosian Desert?
- How did Alexander motivate his soldiers when they found a small amount of water in the desert?
- What steps did Alexander take to fix problems in his empire after reaching Babylon?

- Why did Alexander organize a massive wedding event for his soldiers in Babylon?

- What were some of Alexander's plans for expanding his empire after returning to Babylon?

Governing an Empire

Alexander stood at the heart of the largest empire the world had ever seen. From Greece to Egypt and all the way to Central Asia, his territories stretched across thousands of miles. But conquering all that land was one thing—ruling it was an entirely different challenge. How do you manage so many people who speak different languages and have their own ways of life? Alexander had a plan.

A Leader with a Big Idea

Alexander believed that if his empire was going to survive, everyone needed to feel like they belonged. He couldn't just demand loyalty; he had to earn it. So, he came up with an idea: blend Greek culture with the customs of the people he had conquered. He thought that combining the best parts of each culture would create something strong and unique.

He started by spreading Greek ideas, like philosophy, art, and science, across his empire. Schools were built to teach the Greek language and knowledge. In Persia, Egypt, and beyond, you could hear people discussing ideas from Greek thinkers like Aristotle (who had been Alexander's teacher!). But Alexander didn't stop there. He also adopted the traditions of the people he ruled. For example, he wore Persian clothes and participated in local ceremonies. This showed people that he respected their cultures, too.

Building Bridges Between Worlds

One of Alexander's smartest moves was encouraging his soldiers to marry women from the regions they had conquered. It was a way to create connections between the Greeks and the local people. These unions helped unite his diverse empire.

But Alexander didn't just focus on relationships. He knew that his empire needed strong communication and transportation to stay connected. Imagine trying to send a message from Greece to India without proper roads! Alexander ordered the construction of roads, bridges, and ports to make travel faster and safer. Traders, soldiers, and messengers could now move across the empire more easily, which helped keep things running smoothly.

A Network of Cities

Alexander loved founding cities. Wherever his army went, he made sure to build a city—or improve an existing one. These cities became centers of learning, trade, and culture. They weren't just for Greeks, though. Alexander wanted them to be welcoming places for everyone in his empire.

One of his most famous cities was Alexandria in Egypt. It had a grand library filled with scrolls from all over the world and a bustling marketplace where people from different lands traded goods and stories. Cities like Alexandria helped blend Greek culture with local traditions, creating something entirely new and exciting.

Making Fair Rules

Ruling such a large empire wasn't easy,

especially when it came to keeping the peace. Alexander understood that he needed fair rules so people wouldn't feel mistreated. He worked to create laws that respected the customs of each region while also bringing in Greek ideas of justice.

He appointed governors to oversee different parts of the empire. These leaders were chosen not only from his Greek allies but also from the local population. By giving people from conquered regions important roles, Alexander showed that they were part of the empire, not just outsiders.

Challenges of Being in Charge

Of course, ruling such a vast empire wasn't all smooth sailing. There were rebellions and disagreements. Some people didn't like the idea of mixing cultures, especially among

Alexander's own soldiers. They wanted to stick to Greek traditions and didn't understand why Alexander was embracing foreign ways.

Alexander faced these challenges head-on. He explained his vision of a united empire where everyone worked together. Even though not everyone agreed with him, his determination inspired many to follow his lead.

A Vision Bigger Than Himself

Alexander didn't just think about his empire in the present; he dreamed of the future. He planned to explore lands even farther east, create new cities, and bring more people into his vision of a united world. Unfortunately, his untimely death meant that many of his plans would never come to life.

But the ideas he introduced—like blending cultures and building strong connections between distant regions—had a lasting impact. His empire set an example of how different people could come together to create something greater than themselves.

A Legacy of Unity

Alexander's policies weren't perfect, and not everything went as planned. But his efforts to govern such a vast and diverse empire were groundbreaking. He showed that leadership wasn't just about power; it was about understanding, respect, and vision.

Through his mix of Greek culture and local traditions, he created a unique blend that shaped history. His cities, roads, and ideas became the foundation for future civilizations, proving that sometimes the greatest victories happen not on the battlefield but in the way we connect and work with others.

Questions

- Why did Alexander encourage his soldiers to marry women from the regions they had conquered?

- What was the purpose of building roads, bridges, and ports across Alexander's empire?

- How did the city of Alexandria in Egypt become an important center of culture and learning?

- What was Alexander's approach to making laws for his vast empire?

- How did Alexander handle challenges and disagreements about mixing Greek traditions with local customs?

Alexander's Final Days

Alexander the Great had done what many thought was impossible. He had created one of the largest empires the world had ever seen. But even the greatest of heroes face challenges they cannot overcome.

A Sudden Illness in Babylon

Alexander returned to Babylon, a city he had planned to make the heart of his empire. It was a buzzing hub of activity, filled with traders, scholars, and craftsmen from all corners of his vast lands. Alexander was brimming with plans. He wanted to push further east, explore new lands, and build even more incredible cities. But fate had other ideas.

One evening, during a grand feast with his friends and generals, Alexander suddenly fell ill. At first, everyone thought it was nothing serious. After all, Alexander was known for his incredible strength and endurance. But as the days went by, his condition grew worse. He was burning with fever and struggling to move or speak.

Doctors from all over the empire rushed to his side, but no one could figure out what was wrong. Some whispered that the heat of Babylon had taken its toll. Others suspected he might have caught a disease during his travels. There were even rumors of poison—could someone have betrayed the great Alexander?

Theories About His Death

Alexander passed away after days of suffering. He was only 32 years old. The entire empire was plunged into shock and sorrow. How could someone so powerful, so full of life, be gone so suddenly?

Even today, historians and scientists debate the cause of Alexander's death. Some believe he died of natural causes, like malaria or typhoid, diseases that were common at the time. Others think he may have suffered from an illness brought on by exhaustion from his endless campaigns. His body had endured years of battles, harsh weather, and injuries.

And then there's the theory of poison. Was there someone in Alexander's inner circle who wanted to see him fall? It's a thrilling mystery, but many experts doubt this theory because poisons of that time wouldn't have acted so slowly.

No one knows for sure, and that's part of what makes Alexander's story so fascinating. It leaves us wondering: what really happened to the man who had conquered the world?

The Legacy of a Legend

When Alexander died, he left behind an empire that stretched from Greece to India. But there was one big problem—he had no clear successor. Alexander had a young son, but the boy was too little to rule such a massive empire. Alexander's generals, who had fought alongside him for years, began to argue about what should happen next.

Before his death, Alexander was said to have been asked who should inherit his empire. His answer? "To the strongest." This simple phrase sparked chaos. Instead of uniting under one leader, his generals divided the empire into pieces, each claiming a part for themselves.

The Empire Divided

The division of Alexander's empire marked the end of a united rule. The territories were split into regions known as the Hellenistic Kingdoms, named after the Greek culture Alexander had spread. Here's what happened:

- **Ptolemy** took control of Egypt and founded a dynasty that ruled for centuries. One of its most famous rulers was Cleopatra, who came long after Alexander's time.

- **Seleucus** gained much of Persia and parts of Asia.

- **Antigonus** claimed Macedonia and Greece, although he faced constant challenges from rivals.

The generals, now kings of their own territories, often fought with each other.

Wars broke out, and the unity Alexander had worked so hard to create began to crumble. Even so, the influence of his conquests lived on.

Alexander's Enduring Influence

Alexander's dream of blending cultures didn't fade completely. In the cities he founded, like Alexandria in Egypt, Greek ideas mixed with local traditions. These cities became centers of learning, art, and trade. Scientists, philosophers, and mathematicians thrived in the environment Alexander had set in motion.

One of the most remarkable parts of Alexander's legacy was the spread of the Greek language. It became a common tongue in many parts of his former empire, making communication and trade easier across vast distances.

Alexander also inspired countless leaders and warriors throughout history. His bravery, determination, and ability to think outside the box during battles became legendary. Even today, people look to his story for lessons about leadership and ambition.

The Man Behind the Myth

Though Alexander achieved so much, he was also human. He made mistakes and faced doubts. Not everyone agreed with his methods, and some of his actions, like the burning of Persepolis, were criticized even in his time. But whether you see him as a hero or a flawed leader, there's no denying his impact on history.

Alexander's final days in Babylon are a powerful ending to an incredible story. His life shows how far vision and determination can take someone, even in the face of impossible odds. His empire may not have lasted, but the ideas and culture he spread shaped the world for centuries.

A Mystery for the Ages

Alexander's sudden death, his grand ambitions, and the empire he left behind have made him a subject of endless fascination. What would have happened if he had lived longer? Would he have conquered more lands? Or would he have focused on strengthening the empire he already had?

Though his story ended in Babylon, Alexander's name continues to echo throughout history. He was a warrior, a leader, and a dreamer who dared to reach for the impossible. His life may have been short, but his impact was nothing less than extraordinary.

And so, the story of Alexander the Great comes to an end, not with a quiet farewell but with a legacy that continues to inspire.

He showed the world what it means to aim high, push boundaries, and leave a mark that lasts forever.

Questions

- Where did Alexander plan to make the heart of his empire before his death?
- What mysterious event happened to Alexander during a feast in Babylon?
- What were some theories about the cause of Alexander's death?
- How was Alexander's empire divided after his death, and who were some of the generals involved?
- What cultural and historical impact did Alexander leave behind through the cities he founded?

The Legend of Alexander

After Alexander the Great passed away in 323 BCE, his name did not fade away with him. In fact, it grew stronger, becoming legendary. Stories, myths, and tales about his conquests spread far and wide, and people from different cultures began to add their own spin to the hero they had heard of. His influence extended not only in his own time but for centuries to come.

The Stories and Myths

As with any great leader, the tales about Alexander grew larger than life. Many stories were told about his bravery, wisdom, and daring feats. Some people believed he was almost invincible. Legends say that

Alexander never lost a battle, and though that's not exactly true, the myth of his unbeatable nature was powerful.

One of the most famous myths was about the Gordian Knot. It was said that anyone who could untie the knot, which had been a puzzle for generations, would rule all of Asia. Alexander, in true fashion, didn't waste time trying to untie it with his hands. Instead, he took his sword and sliced the knot in half, symbolizing his bold and unconventional approach to problems. This story turned him into a figure of not just military might but also cleverness and daring.

Influence on Later Leaders

Alexander's story did not stop with his death. The legend of his greatness would inspire some of history's most famous leaders, like Julius Caesar and Napoleon Bonaparte.

Julius Caesar, the Roman general and statesman, admired Alexander greatly. In fact, it's said that when Caesar visited Alexander's tomb, he wept, feeling that he had not accomplished as much in his life as Alexander had by the time he was his age. Caesar, who would go on to conquer much of Europe, looked up to Alexander as a role model, and his ambitions were fueled by Alexander's example.

Napoleon Bonaparte, another famous conqueror, was also deeply inspired by Alexander. Napoleon, who aimed to build his own empire, saw Alexander as the ultimate figure of military success. He studied Alexander's campaigns and even tried to follow in his footsteps by conquering large parts of Europe and Egypt. Napoleon believed that to be a great leader, one had to think as Alexander did: boldly, decisively, and always forward-looking.

How He's Remembered in History and Culture

Alexander's legacy didn't just stay in the minds of military leaders. His name is known around the world, and his influence can be seen in art, literature, and even in the names of cities. Cities like Alexandria in Egypt and others across Asia and Europe were founded by Alexander or named in his honor. These cities became important cultural hubs and spread Greek culture far and wide, creating what we now call the Hellenistic Era.

The Hellenistic Era was a time when Greek ideas, art, and architecture blended with the cultures of the regions Alexander conquered. People began to see the world in a new way, sharing knowledge and ideas that crossed borders. Alexander didn't just conquer lands—he connected people.

In art and literature, Alexander became a symbol of greatness. Writers and historians, both in the ancient world and later, wrote books and plays about him. In fact, one of the most famous ancient books about Alexander is The Alexander Romance, a collection of stories filled with both historical facts and thrilling legends about his life and deeds. This book spread across many cultures and was translated into several languages, making Alexander's story known to generations of readers.

Alexander's Enduring Popularity

Even to this day, Alexander's story continues to captivate people all over the world. His life is filled with adventure, drama, and triumph, making it the perfect tale for movies, books, and even video games. He's not just a figure from ancient history—he's a part of the popular imagination.

Historians and scholars continue to study his life, trying to understand the full impact of his achievements. But beyond the facts and figures, what makes Alexander truly legendary is how his story has lived on through centuries, inspiring people to dream big and act boldly.

The Man Behind the Legend

Though many myths surround him, we can't forget that Alexander was a real person—a king, a general, and a visionary. He wasn't just a military genius; he was also a man with big dreams and an unyielding desire to push beyond what was thought possible. His life wasn't easy, and he faced many challenges, from the loss of close friends to the long, exhausting battles that took a toll on his army. But through it all, his spirit of determination and his vision of a world united by culture and knowledge continued to drive him forward.

The legend of Alexander is more than just the story of a king who conquered the world. It's about the way his ideas shaped the future, inspiring generations to think bigger and to believe in their own potential. Whether as a fearless leader, a strategic genius, or a symbol of ambition, Alexander the Great's story is far from over. His name lives on as a symbol of what can be achieved when we dare to dream and never stop moving forward.

Questions

- How did Alexander's story inspire later leaders like Julius Caesar and Napoleon?
- What was the Gordian Knot legend, and how did Alexander handle it?
- How did Alexander influence the cultures of the regions he conquered?
- What was the Hellenistic Era, and how is it connected to Alexander's conquests?

- Why do people still talk about Alexander the Great today?

What Can We Learn from Alexander the Great?

Alexander the Great wasn't just a famous conqueror; he was a leader, a dreamer, and someone who believed that anything was possible. His story is filled with lessons that can inspire all of us. Even though he lived over 2,000 years ago, his journey still has something to teach us today, especially about leadership, ambition, perseverance, and the power of thinking big.

Leadership: Leading with Confidence

One of the most amazing things about Alexander was his ability to lead his army to victory again and again. He wasn't just a general sitting safely behind the lines—he was right there with his soldiers, leading the charge. Imagine having a leader who goes through the same struggles as you and fights side by side with you. That's what Alexander did. His soldiers loved him for it, and they trusted him completely.

But leadership isn't just about being brave in battle. It's also about making decisions, even when they're tough. For example, when his army was tired and wanted to go home, Alexander didn't give up. He pushed forward, always thinking of the bigger picture. He showed that a true leader is someone who motivates others, listens to their team, and keeps going, even when things get tough. He didn't just tell his army what to do—he showed them what could be achieved with hard work and determination.

Ambition: Dream Big, Dream Bold

Alexander was a master of ambition. From a young age, he dreamed big. He didn't just want to rule his home country, Macedonia; he wanted to rule the world. And guess what? He didn't stop until he achieved it. His dream wasn't just about power—it was about bringing people from different places together and creating something bigger than anyone had ever imagined before.

We can learn from Alexander that it's okay to dream big. Maybe your dreams are about becoming a scientist, an artist, or an athlete. Just like Alexander, you can set your sights on something amazing and work towards it. Ambition isn't about being the best or the first; it's about pushing yourself to achieve your goals, no matter how big or small. The important thing is to keep aiming high and believe that with enough effort, anything is possible.

Perseverance: Never Give Up

One of Alexander's most important qualities was his perseverance. His journey wasn't easy—he had to face enormous challenges. His army traveled through deserts, climbed mountains, and fought fierce enemies. Sometimes, things got so tough that his soldiers wanted to quit. But Alexander didn't let that happen. He kept them motivated and reminded them of the bigger picture. He believed in his mission so much that he kept moving forward, even when the odds seemed impossible.

Perseverance is one of the most important lessons we can learn from Alexander. Whether you're learning to play an instrument, studying for a test, or practicing a sport, things might not always go the way you want. But like Alexander, if you keep trying and don't give up, you'll eventually see progress. The key is to push through the difficult times and believe that you can achieve what you set out to do. Challenges are part of the journey, and overcoming them is what makes success feel so rewarding.

Cultural Exchange: Bringing the World Together

While Alexander is often remembered for his military victories, there was another side to his legacy that's just as important. He believed in the idea of blending cultures. As he traveled and conquered new lands, Alexander didn't just force people to follow his ways. Instead, he encouraged them to share their cultures and ideas. He founded cities where people from different parts of the world could live together, and he promoted the idea of cultural exchange. This wasn't just about conquering; it was about learning from each other and creating a world where different traditions and ideas could come together.

Alexander's vision shows us the power of learning from people who are different from us. When we open our minds and hearts to different cultures, we can grow in ways we never imagined. We can learn new things, see the world from different perspectives, and become more understanding and respectful of others. It's a reminder that diversity is something to be celebrated, not feared.

Thinking Big: Don't Limit Yourself

One of the biggest things we can learn from Alexander is the power of thinking big. He didn't limit himself to what was easy or familiar—he dreamed about a world that no one else had ever imagined. Alexander believed in creating something so big and bold that it would change the world forever.

You don't have to conquer the world to think big. Maybe your big dream is to invent something new, start a business, write a book, or make a positive impact in your community. Just like Alexander, you can set your sights high and think beyond what's possible. If you believe in yourself and stay focused, you can achieve things that others might think are impossible.

Encouragement to Chase Your Dreams

Now, you might be thinking, "But I'm just a kid! What can I do?" The truth is, you're never too young to dream big and work hard to make those dreams a reality. Alexander was young when he started his journey, and just like him, you have the power to set your goals and start working towards them today. Whether it's learning a new skill, being kind to others, or trying your best in everything you do, each step you take brings you closer to your dreams.

Don't let anyone tell you your dreams are too big or that you're too young to make a difference. Alexander's story is proof that if you have the passion, the will, and the perseverance, you can achieve great things. It might not happen overnight, but with dedication and a positive mindset, you can reach for the stars.

Final Thoughts: What's Your Legacy?

Alexander's life is a story of ambition, leadership, and a vision that changed the world. But it's also a story of one person who believed that anything was possible. He didn't settle for what was easy or familiar—he pushed himself to new heights, and in doing so, he made an impact on the world that lasted for thousands of years.

What about you? What can you learn from Alexander the Great? What big dreams do you want to chase? Just like Alexander, you have the power to create your own legacy, to leave your mark on the world. So go ahead, dream big, work hard, and never give up. Your adventure is just beginning.

Questions

- How did Alexander show leadership during his campaigns?
- Why is ambition important, and how did Alexander's ambition help him succeed?
- What role did perseverance play in Alexander's journey?
- How did Alexander promote cultural exchange, and what can we learn from that?
- What big dreams do you have, and how can you start working toward them today?

CONCLUSION

Alexander the Great's journey wasn't just about winning battles or conquering lands—it was about dreaming big and having the courage to turn those dreams into reality. His story shows that no goal is too big if you have the vision and determination to chase it. Along the way, he faced enormous challenges, but his leadership, creativity, and willingness to learn from others helped him build an empire that changed the world.

Looking back at Alexander's life, we can take away important lessons that will guide us in our own adventures. Whether it's through leadership, building new friendships, or simply believing in ourselves when things get tough, his example encourages us to be bold, stay focused, and never stop striving for what we want.

Alexander's legacy proves that anyone—no matter how young or where they come from—can make an impact. So, just like Alexander, chase your dreams, embrace new opportunities, and know that the world is full of possibilities waiting for you to explore. Your adventure is just getting started!

Explore More!

Albert Einstein
Book for Curious Kids
E=mc²
MARK LYLANI
SCAN ME
NIKOLA TESLA
BOOK FOR CURIOUS KIDS
TIMOTHY STARLYN
SCAN ME
Eugenie Clark
Book for Curious Kids
ERIC LYLANI
SCAN ME

Made in United States
Troutdale, OR
04/11/2025

30531661R10116